The Irish Theatre Series 9
Edited by Robert Hogan, James Kilroy *and* Liam Miller

The Dublin Drama League

GW00372926

The Dublin Drama League

1918-1941

by Brenna Katz Clarke and Harold Ferrar

The Dolmen Press

Humanities Press Inc.

Contents

Set in Times Roman type
and printed and published in the Republic of Ireland
at The Dolmen Press, North Richmond Street, Dublin 1

First published 1979

Distributed in North America by Humanities Press Inc.
171 First Avenue, Atlantic Highlands, N.J. 07716

ISBN 0 85105 316 5

Grateful acknowledgment is made to the Director and staff of the
National Library of Ireland for their tireless help.

Foreword

This little study came about mostly by accident. One summer's Dublin day I was browsing through the bound volumes of the Abbey Theatre programmes in the National Library when I noticed a volume tucked behind the others at the end of the shelf. It turned out to be Joseph Holloway's collection of more than half of the programmes of the Dublin Drama League. I leafed through the book with increasing excitement as the names of so many of the renowned Abbey actors appeared in programme after programme in plays by nearly every major modern dramatist. I knew a bit about the Drama League from my research for a previous book on the plays of Denis Johnston but my restricted interests had prevented me from recognizing that a very vigorous and provocative theatre had been striving throughout the 'twenties to expand the domain of Irish arts. As I began to grasp the scope of the League's efforts, I suddenly felt an obligation to reconstruct what I could of its history. I was both delighted in my find and alarmed that the League's record had been entrusted so long to a dusty book that at any second could slip forever out of sight.

It didn't take very long for me to lose my perspective — that loss which makes scholarship possible and which has long been fair game for the *farceur*. The League loomed before me as the missing link that miraculously clarified the entire evolution of Irish drama. I ran headlong back to Yeats's letters and biographies, to the many studies of the Abbey, to Lady Gregory's journals and to Lennox Robinson's memoirs; nowhere did I find more than passing reference to the League.

I shared my discovery with another American Gaelophile, Brenna Katz Clarke, and together we blew the dust and wiped the mould from unfittable volumes of crumbling newspapers, then we interviewed everyone we could locate who had been active in the League. Our work was entirely a labour of love and we hope it will properly establish the too long neglected real significance of the League without sacrificing the burst of energy and fun in which it was conceived.

There are too few theatre people remaining from that golden age. This book is for them, and also for all those who have given us a joyous Irish theatre to cherish.

Harold Ferrar

For Derek and Jessica
Thou hast a lap full of seed

and for Ray and Rachel

The Dublin Drama League

I

If one reads through the issues of *Beltaine* and *Samhain*, Yeats's theatre magazines which appeared during the formative years of the Abbey, there can be no mistaking the intention of the Abbey's founders to include non-Irish plays in the repertory. While the over-riding goal was to nurture a substantial native dramatic art where there had been none before, productions of continental plays were to be a minor but steady second line in the theatrical front of the cultural campaign we now call the Irish Literary Renaissance. Yeats was keenly aware of the dangers inherent in the exclusive fostering of Irish arts; he shared Russell's concern: 'We must penetrate the Irish culture with world wisdom or it will cease to be a culture.' Turn, however, to the history of the Abbey's first twenty years and you will find just three full-length and two one-act contemporary European plays out of nearly two hundred Abbey productions. The work of Ibsen, Wedekind, Schnitzler, Chekhov, Gorki and all the advances of the stage's resources accomplished by the free theatre movement remained unknown in Dublin. What happened to that initial plan to open Irish theatre not only inward to its own splendid national potential but outward as well to the teeming excitement beyond its borders?

To begin with, no one could have predicted the magnificent response to the call for a new Irish drama. Lady Gregory has said that she 'had from the beginning a vision of . . . plays being sent to us through all the counties of Ireland'. That vision was to come true more wonderfully than even the Abbey creators could have imagined in their most euphoric moments. J. M. Synge, Padraic Colum, Lennox Robinson, T. C. Murray, St. John Ervine; Lady Gregory and Yeats themselves — an array of talents rising seemingly out of nowhere almost all at once to build a never to be forgotten, genuinely Irish theatre. And just over the horizon, still to arrive in Yeats's lifetime, were Sean O'Casey, Brinsley Mac Namara, George Shiels, Denis Johnston, Paul Vincent Carroll, Teresa Deevy and Frank O'Connor. And this extraordinary flowering of Irish playwrights went hand in hand with a bevy of great

7

performing talents: the Fays, Sara Allgood, Arthur Sinclair, Fred O'Donovan and later Arthur Shields, May Craig, Barry Fitzgerald, Shelah Delany, F. J. McCormick, Shelah Richards. To keep the theatre alive there was no need to go beyond Ireland herself. Thus, while the production of foreign plays had been a sincere but distinctly secondary aim, it was virtually forgotten in the Abbey's shining triumph.

But perhaps the explanation is not so simple and happy. Other factors, symptomatic of the early presence of backstage tensions and conflicts between personalities and purposes, were involved in the scant attention paid to non-Irish drama. Even the Abbey's chief justification for existence — the Irishness of the enterprise — was fraught with hostility from the beginning. There had been instant Catholic protest over *The Countess Cathleen*, the play that launched the new Irish theatre. The actors for the first few years had been imported from England (since a country without a heritage of drama had no actors waiting in the wings) and this necessity was seen by some as proof irrefutable that the nationalist thrust was sham. How could Protestant ascendancy figures like Yeats, Lady Gregory, George Moore, or a wealthy Catholic land-owner with vested interests like Edward Martyn be in touch with the mainstream of the Catholic Ireland they sought to revive? Such were the bitter indictments of hypersensitive Irish Ireland betrayed before the fact. From its inception the Abbey had to wage 'the day's war with ev'ry knave and dolt'. Among fervent nationalists frustrated by military impotence against Britain and having to settle temporarily for verbal tactics, the Abbey had already been type-cast indelibly as Protestant and esoteric, a characterization antithetical to the founders' purpose but one which they never were able to shake completely. Malice, malcomprehension, distrust and hasty condemnation seem to be the constant companions of Irish initiative. Weren't the rebels of Easter, 1916, met with them as surely as the Abbey directorate?

The hysterical xenophobia of the 'rabblement' and the rancour of political disappointment which could be relied upon to dog every artistic step forward were unfortunately bolstered by restless dissension within the ranks. The kind of internal stress that erupted so fiercely in the *Playboy* and *The Plough and the Stars* contro-versies was always stirring in less violent form. A faction of the first native actors of the company deeply resented the subsidy accepted in 1903 from the English tea heiress Miss A. E. F. Horni-man, though without it the theatre was doomed. For the dissidents,

8

it would have been better to do without theatre than to accept an Irish theatre on an English dole. The same group felt that, far from concerning itself with European material, the Abbey wasn't Irish enough. Its money was English, their argument went, its language was English, and it ceased to be amateur and belong truly to the people when it began to pay salaries with Miss Horniman's gift. So in 1905, led by Máire Nic Shiubhlaigh, several actors defected to form the Irish language Theatre of Ireland. If its very Irishness was suspect and under constant surveillance, what could the Abbey expect if it inaugurated productions of non-Irish works? Not that the pressures of jingoism or mindlessness or discontent within the company would have stopped Yeats if he felt European work must be done as a matter of artistic principle. But obviously priority had to be given to fighting more urgent battles, like the education of an audience to welcome the unnerving genius of Synge. (Ironically, Miss Horniman withdrew her support in 1910 because the Abbey was *too* Irish and, with what she considered unforgiveable disrespect, had performed on the day of Edward VII's funeral.)

The ongoing quest for native material, the public's responses, the split within the company were all cardinal factors in the Abbey's formative period. But predominant in the casting of the theatre's goals and in the fixing of its core of permanent identity were the personalities and relationship of Yeats and Lady Gregory. In what we can piece together of their shared and diverging dreams of a rejuvenated Irish culture and of their professional association we can find many of the underlying causes for the Abbey's line of growth.

Lady Gregory, who rapidly emerged as the strong, business-minded force, was inclined to keep the Abbey on a strict Irish diet. She held a hard-line position on the exclusion of European plays, particularly distasteful modern ones which smacked of the *avant-garde* or reeked of late nineteenth-century urban realism. The national theatre was to be a people's theatre: poetic, inspirational, close to the mystical feeling for the Irish soil, fed by heroic myth, folklore and the simple, true life of the countryside. Her transplantation of Molière and Goldoni into Irish country comedies was in line with her original objectives. But the daring continental experiments of the day, most of which were dangerously sexual anyway, had no place on her Irish stage. The new psychological explorations may have been geographically separated from Ireland by only two narrow bodies of water but they were light years away

9

from the needs of this agrarian, ecclesiastical, and subjugated nation. The Abbey was first and foremost a political theatre, a step in the complex movement towards self-determination which can only be forged on an unshakeable base of national pride. The struggle for artistic freedom to plummet the dark recesses of the psyche was to be fought much later in Ireland. The business at hand was to foster a self-sustaining theatre which would be a prime agent in a revolution of national consciousness. Lady Gregory's basic theatrical conservatism surfaced unmistakeably in the 'twenties when European forms were beginning to interest Irish playwrights and when she insisted the Abbey reject a fine modernist play like *The Old Lady Says 'No!'*. Her tenacity was essential to the theatre's survival through the financial crises, internecine strains and the depressions that followed the vicious attacks in the early days. But later, when the original Irish impetus had long proven itself, Æ's fear of a self-devouring hermeticism began to seem prophetic as freshness deteriorated in formula and the Abbey seemed stuck on what Gabriel Fallon called a treadmill of peasant plays. At this point, Lady Gregory's 'powerful character' and conservative bias became counter-productive. Many reservoirs of 'the Irish thing' had been exhausted by the mid-teens and the terrible years of the Troubles and Civil War had not yet opened new watersheds of Irish experience. Several actors and playwrights began to voice an impatient cry for new stimuli and wider horizons.

Yeats, as devoted to an Irish theatre as Lady Gregory, was more sensitive to these changing needs. He was less worried about the hardiness of the Abbey's Irish tradition and was able to imagine deviations from its format which would not fracture it irreparably. He did however share Lady Gregory's distaste for the turn of the century continental vogue of 'spiritless' realism which erroneously paraded as the legacy of Ibsen (as a result, Dublin had to wait until 1924, eighteen years after the death of the major figure in modern world drama, to see an Ibsen 'social' play). But Yeats was very receptive to the symbolist heritage of the school of *Axel*. In the early 1900s Yeats was writing his own mystical plays like *The Shadowy Waters*, and in keeping with this phase of his work, the first modern play in translation performed at the Abbey was Maeterlinck's *The Interior* (1907).

This was an isolated instance, not the beginning of a trend. Ireland was always foremost in Yeats's Abbey dream, and he and Lady Gregory were in near perfect harmony during the critical formative period of the first years of this century. He was deeply absorbed in productions of her 'wonder' plays and, above all, he was overseeing the work of Synge, an undertaking he recognized as the acid test of the Abbey's worth as a national theatre and as the fulfillment of his own dramatic ideas. Frank O'Connor insists, we think rightly, that the *Playboy's* fate struck at the heart of Yeats's dream of an Irish theatre. It left a hidden but unhealed wound of futility. Yeats continued zestfully to play the leading role at the Abbey for a quarter of a century after the death of Synge, and he strove tirelessly to protect and extend the Abbey's achievement. Thus, his relationship to the theatre which would never have been born without him became tragically ambivalent after Synge's death. Proper recognition has not been given to his personal heroism in remaining loyal to a theatre that grew so one-sided it had little room for the plays of its greatest figure.

Despite repeated disappointments, Yeats continued to plan moves that would re-awaken the primal fire. In 1910, for instance, with his typical lightning enthusiasm he convinced the directorate that Lennox Robinson, a 24-year-old Cork writer (who had written a one-acter for the Abbey) was the whiteheaded boy to set the Abbey back on the road to glory. Thanks to Yeats, the Abbey found the man who not only was to become its most frequent director, but who was to be responsible for bringing European drama to Ireland.

Later, in the 'thirties, when the Abbey suffered its most critical period as Yeats took a progressively less active role, Robinson became a cramping agent subtly biased toward uninspired revival of time-tested popular work. But for twenty years, 1910–1930, Robinson manipulated his influential position as Yeats's protege with great skill, striving constantly and successfully for a world perspective in Irish theatre. Naturally he had to step gingerly at first, especially since Lady Gregory quickly and permanently disapproved of him, and he found himself awkwardly having to convince Yeats to oppose her without Yeats seeming to be a mere middleman too blindly committed to the outlook of his youthful discovery.

Robinson managed almost instantly to move Yeats towards his international viewpoint, and a production of *Little Eyolf*, one of Ibsen's least socially-oriented plays, drenched with the kind of private demonic mythology Yeats adored, was in rehearsal in the autumn of 1910 when it had to be suddenly scrapped to make way for T. C. Murray's first Abbey play. Then in 1913 Robinson produced four contemporary non-Irish works: Hauptmann's *Hannele*, Strindberg's *There are Crimes and Crimes* and *The Stronger*, and

The Post Office by the Indian playwright Tagore — none of them in the realistic mode, hence acceptable to Yeats. But this brief flurry proved to be only that and the Abbey allowed no more of this kind of thing until 1921; one senses the hand of Lady Gregory firmly steering the theatre back onto her chart of its proper journey. Robinson never succeeded during Yeats's tenure in establishing the production of foreign plays as a regular part of the Abbey's offerings. It was abundantly clear by the mid-teens that the Abbey was simply not the place for an ongoing international repertory, and perhaps rightly so. An alternative outside the Abbey was the only solution and Robinson started a brilliant one in 1918, a little theatre that was to have an immeasurably benevolent impact on the Irish drama in the 'twenties and 'thirties: the Dublin Drama League.

II

The Drama League was Lennox Robinson's brainchild, but it would never have grown beyond the embryo stage without the strong backing of James Stephens, of Ernest Boyd, the literary historian, and above all of Yeats who served as the League's president until 1926. In the autumn of 1918, when Robinson was fervently enlisting financial and ideological support for the experimental venture, the Irish political situation was explosive. World War I was cooling off and the Irish troubles were heating up. As the anti-British guerrilla strategy intensified, it began to dawn on the Irish people, whose allegiances had been so sharply cleaved during the war years, that after centuries of fantasizing, brave words were finally becoming deeds. A genuine, broad-based movement toward Irish liberty was underway, and Irish pride was rampant. We have seen that the Abbey's Irishness was constantly distrusted by a vociferous chauvinist fringe, and that what the founders considered a people's theatre was to its opponents an Anglo-Irish coterie theatre geared to the happy few of the intelligentsia. To turn then towards Europe at this particular moment was courageous for both Robinson and for the Abbey, which recognized its own incapacity to provide broader theatrical perspectives and supported the Drama League's efforts. Pleading for initial subscriptions to the Drama League, Robinson found it necessary to assure the public in advance that the League would not subvert the new rise in the nationalist tide: 'Here in Ireland we are isolated, cut off from the thought of the world, except the English world, and from England we get little in drama, except fourth-rate. I ask you, for the young writer's sake, to open the door. . . . Seeing foreign plays will not divorce our minds from Ireland.' Yeats naturally understood the fertile possibilities for the future thrust of Irish arts inherent in a project like the League. Lady Gregory was openly hostile at first, then soon fell into disapproving silence; her name is conspicuously absent from any association with the League's history.

Robinson's concept was unique in that the League was managed by its audience-subscriber members who determined policy, elected officers, chose a play selection committee, and formed a committee to negotiate for presentations by visiting companies. The Abbey agreed to make its stage available for a small fee on Sunday and Monday nights when there were no scheduled Abbey performances (Yeats was undoubtedly the prime mover in this decision) and Abbey personnel were free to participate in the League. It soon became possible to see, say, F. J. McCormick in a George Shiels's country comedy one night and in a Pirandello role the next, and to be treated to some real-life drama like a frisking up against a wall on the way home from the Abbey during those violent days when theatregoing could be hazardous and the attendance was sparse.

With its first production on 9 February 1919, the Drama League proclaimed its identity loudly and clearly. The play, Srgjan Tucic's *The Liberators*, was destined for instant oblivion. But it was a rich, and in the overall Irish context, an enormously welcome statement of purpose. This particular play lived for a moment and was gone forever but it announced the arrival of a theatre which dared, from the outset, to desert the security of the dominant peasant play. The League's first choice was an obscure Bulgarian anti war piece contemporary, timely and serious. Plainly the League intended to fulfil an obligation basic to the imaginative life of the theatre; it would not play safe. As one sympathetic critic later put it, the League's business was not to court success but to produce brilliant failures.

The programme of the first production included a list of officers, a membership application for the year at 18s. 6d., and a description of the threefold implementation of the League's goal, 'to secure the production of plays, which, in the ordinary course of events, would not be likely to be seen in Dublin. Such production may be achieved in three ways: Companies on tour with a play the League

13

wished to see might be attracted to Dublin by a guarantee; existing companies in Dublin might be asked by the League to produce a play in return for the League's support; the League might commission a producer in Dublin to present a particular play for them.' While the League eventually sponsored an appearance of the Birmingham Repertory company's production of Pirandello's *Six Characters*, its own productions quickly became the League's reason for being as it planned six public and two at-home programmes annually.

The achievements of the League were remarkable. In its active decade (1919–1929) it produced sixty-six plays written originally in eleven languages by thirty-six authors from fifteen countries, using nearly twenty directors and over half-a-dozen designers. It gave would-be translators a chance to try their hands and Abbey actors who weren't performing could watch their colleagues in roles that sharply burst the confines of usual repertory familiarity. Amateurs too were eagerly encouraged to participate; a group of them which came to be known as the 'Dramick' presented material informally during the at-homes for the League's consideration for regular scheduling. The League was never subsidized and had always to pay its own way, yet under all circumstances it maintained a sincere professionalism and always paid its actors decently. Gabriel Fallon thinks the clearest indication of the effectiveness of the League's 'audience-organised' format was the fact that when it finally dissolved it ended up with a £20 bank balance. Some of the League's efforts may have been raggedy-edged (though six of them were impressive enough to be taken over for runs at the Abbey), and some were rapidly thrown together under difficult conditions since first commitments were to the Abbey, or in the case of amateurs, to jobs. Lady Gleneavy (Beatrice Campbell, one of the League's designers) has a cartoon in her scrapbook depicting a room in her home where Denis Johnston and his first wife Shelah Richards are preparing for a League play while one of the Gleneavy children is doing schoolwork and another is brandishing a golf club and complaining 'nuff talk'. Good humour, exuberance and a measure of frustration characterized the League, which is remembered with affection and gratitude by people like Johnston, Richards and the late Sybil Le Brocquy. Johnston summed up the League's value to the Dublin theatre world: 'Lennox and the Drama League really did remarkable work in introducing to Dublin all the *avant-garde* plays of the time. . . . He taught us and showed us Strindberg, Pirandello, Benavente, Schnitzler — people whose plays we would never have seen — and maybe not even have read, if it hadn't been for the Drama League.'

The rosters of the League's programmes comprise a who's who in Irish drama in the 'twenties and a who was going to be who in the 'thirties. For the League not only offered the established greats of the Abbey opportunities to extend their range, it was as well a spawning ground for a number of young, gifted theatre talents, including some (Denis Johnston is the best-known) whose whole development owes an inestimable debt to experience gained in the League. The League offered myriad opportunities denied by the Abbey because of financial exigencies, public accountability, and a fairly rigid internal hierarchy of seniority. Barry Fitzgerald did his first directing for the League as did Gabriel Fallon, P. J. Carolan, Denis Johnston and Shelah Richards. Conversely, Lennox Robinson, who never once acted at the Abbey appeared in ten roles for the League under the stage name of Paul Ruttledge (the hero of Yeats's play *Where There is Nothing*). He was able to develop this neglected side of his theatre art in such plum roles of the modern repertory as Pirandello's Henry IV and Arkenholz the Student in Strindberg's *Spook Sonata*. Frank O'Connor played for the League, as did Michael Scott who was destined for acclaim as an architect and designer of the new Abbey. Maud Gonne, who had created the role of Cathleen Ni Houlihan in Yeats's most popular play in 1902, returned after eighteen years absence from the Dublin stage to play Hecuba in Euripides' *The Trojan Women*. Sara Allgood returned to Dublin to act and direct for the League; Mary Manning, later a fine dramatist for the Gate, acted at the League, as did the Ulster playwright Rutherford Mayne, and Meriel Moore and Betty Chancellor who became the Gate's leading actresses.

And those everpresent great names remind us how fully the Abbey was interwoven with the League: F. J. McCormick played seventeen League parts, Barry Fitzgerald, Maureen Delany and Eileen Crowe eleven each, Michael J. Dolan fifteen, P. J. Carolan eighteen. Arthur Shields, who was with the League from its first days, played the most roles (nineteen) and directed as often as Robinson. Shields was a keenly intelligent actor and an occasional director for the Abbey, but it was the Drama League that offered him the scope for his gifts, and he developed into a key figure in Dublin's *avant-garde* theatre experimentalism, especially in Expressionism. The Abbey's venerable Seaghan Barlow created a good deal of the scenery for the League, but later some of Ireland's

15

excellent young painters like Norah McGuinness and Louis Le Brocquy began to design productions. These statistical details give us a sense of the variety, the bustle and the excitement generated by the League which in a few seasons made itself an indispensable part of Dublin cultural life. Henry Adams once said that a teacher's influence is not quantitatively measurable but stretches to infinity. The Drama League has never occupied its deservedly honoured place in the history of the Irish theatre, but like Adams's teacher, its prodigious contribution to the growth of the people who made that history is inestimable.

The list of world dramatists performed by the League reads like a hall of fame rollcall: Chekhov, Strindberg, Andreyev, Schnitzler, O'Neill, Brieux, Lenormand, Benavente, the Sierras, Pirandello, Toller, Claudel, Buchner, Euripides, Shaw, Yeats. The League's deliberate eclecticism prevented a lopsided investment in any single style or point of view. Well-made problem plays, realistic regional folk plays, naturalism, classical tragedy, comedy of manners, poetic symbolism, Expressionism, farce; plays as famous as *The Three Sisters* or as unknown as *The Housetop Madman*, a Japanese play never heard of before or since — all had a place in the balance and range which was so essential to the League's effectiveness.

Unlike the flood of Irish plays that poured into the Abbey in its early days, the Drama League did not inspire a sudden outburst of dramatists whose work was shot through with modernist techniques. Yet in addition to the pervasive influence of the League on the overall climate of Irish theatre, it played a direct, traceable part in the careers of a few Irish playwrights. Here the League's openness to Expressionism stands out, thanks to the vision of Shields. Seán O'Casey attended, Fallon estimates, about sixty per cent of the Drama League's plays. His exposure to Strindberg, Andreyev, Toller and O'Neill's early work undoubtedly was a key factor in his turning to very experimental methods in that landmark play in the history of the Irish drama, *The Silver Tassie* (1928). And virtually all his post-exile output continues in this line. The League was also instrumental in the development of one of Ireland's foremost dramatists, Denis Johnston. Shortly after O'Casey's departure Johnston was hailed as the next major Irish playwright. His first play, *The Old Lady Says 'No!'* (1926–29) was also the first Irish Expressionist play, written while Johnston was directing and performing for the League and for the New Players (a League spin-off by members of the Dramick to put on only radically

16

avant-garde plays). Lennox Robinson himself applied in *Church Street* (1934) the lessons he learned from the League's productions of Pirandello.

III

The numerous specific accomplishments of the League are self-evident. There remains however a question for subtler analysis, one which brings us back to our starting point: what was the place of the Drama League in the evolution of Irish drama and particularly what insights does it provide us into the intricate conflicts of Yeats's relationship to the theatre during the latter period of his career.

In the mid-teens, around the time when it seemed the Abbey was hopelessly stalled in the doldrums of the realistic peasant play, Yeats turned towards the Orient and began to write his dance plays. Perhaps he finally abandoned the dream of a perfect marriage between his theatre and his playwriting; at any rate he was at this point experimenting with dramatic forms as uniquely original as any in the modern theatre. It must have been clear to him that they were wholly unsuitable for the sort of theatre the Abbey had become, and from this point on, with a nobly concealed bitterness that he let out only in the last year or two of his life (in *On the Boiler* for instance), he divorced his playwriting from his theatre management. We suspect that his quick readiness to go along with Robinson's plan for the Drama League and to serve as the League's president for eight years was largely due to an immense private disappointment which he would never publicly reveal but which must have caused him great anguish. Yet throughout, Yeats was able to maintain his belief in the Irish identity of the Abbey and his fervour to pass the theatre on as the finest collective achievement of Ireland's literary revival was the source of his unflagging managerial energy and combativeness. We think too his willingness to take positions uncongenial to Lady Gregory, like inviting Denis Johnston to direct an unconventional *King Lear* at the Abbey in 1928, or upholding Robinson's League plan, stemmed from his recognition of the Abbey's failures and from his determination to redeem them as best he could. Sadly, his early passionate ideals had dwindled to a mere holding action, a few attempts to prevent the Abbey from throwing up impenetrable walls around its own shortcomings.

Going into the 'twenties, then, Yeats had a deeply conflicted relationship with the theatre. He still believed the original Irish goals had to remain uppermost, but he wanted to apply them with greater elasticity, allowing, as in the *King Lear* project, for occasional departures from the norm. At the same time he had virtually given up hope that the Abbey would welcome his own new work. His fears were to prove well-founded: from 1919 to 1929 (the active years of the Drama League), the Abbey produced precisely *one* premiere of a new Yeats play, *The Player Queen* in December, 1919. And this came eight years after its previous production of a new Yeats work. Thus the Abbey compiled the appalling record of just one lone Yeats premiere in over eighteen years.

In the mid and later 'twenties, things were as bad at the Abbey as they were in the nation. Political liberty turned instantly to interior discord with no common enemy to unite Irishmen. In terms of sheer violence, history seemed to repeat itself intact during the brutal post-revolutionary decade. Parnell, when he returned to Ireland after his exoneration from the Phoenix Park killings, told a navvy: 'Ireland shall get her freedom and you still break stone.' As O'Casey wrote of the Free State, the only difference now was that Irishmen instead of Englishmen were wearing the top hats and the mail boxes were painted green instead of red. Parnell's prophecy held as true for the national theatre as for the nation. Independence had not cured the prejudice and backbiting of Dublin audiences any more than it had brought peace, unity or prosperity to the country. By the mid-'twenties the Abbey audience had 'disgraced itself again', O'Casey was going into exile, Denis Johnston's first play was rejected, and Yeats's plays were unproduced.

All had to turn elsewhere, for no dramatist can function without seeing what happens to his plays in the theatre. The Drama League eagerly welcomed Yeats's work and produced three of his experimental plays: *The Cat and the Moon, At the Hawk's Well,* and *The Only Jealousy of Emer.* This last was choreographed by Ninette de Valois and designed (scenery and masks) by Norah McGuinness, in a production closely supervised by Yeats. It was the first real opportunity Yeats had to see one of his dance plays performed in a style approaching his conception, and it is the clearest evidence of the League's enormous meaning to him.

Yeats and Robinson tried to carry over to the Abbey the thrust of experiment and the atmosphere of risk and daring that characterized the League. During the 'twenties the Abbey adopted six Drama League productions, four of them in 1926–27 (*Doctor*

Knock by Jules Romains, O'Neill's *The Emperor Jones*, Susan Glaspell's *Trifles* and Shaw's *Caesar and Cleopatra*). This ripple of atypical Abbey presentations was part of a last-ditch struggle by Yeats to shift the Abbey towards a more venturesome course. There were a few other tentative trials: a semi-futuristic production of *King Lear* (the Abbey's first Shakespearean play); the ballets of Ninette de Valois; and the dance version of *Fighting the Waves* with an ultra-modern score by Georges Antheil. These experiments which Yeats managed to bring to the Abbey were fruits of the League's seeds that blossomed for a brief moment and wilted as the Abbey speedily rejected innovation. And with the return to the basic realism of the 'Abbey style' in the 'thirties, Yeats increasingly withdrew from active participation in the theatre. Unable to keep his regret to himself any longer, he pleaded scornfully in the prologue to his last play for an audience of no more than fifty or a hundred to value his dream.

IV

The Drama League did its work so well that Dublin, which had no European drama before the League's inception, was never to be without it afterwards. During the 'twenties, Dublin at last had a vitally needed alternative, a second serious theatre. To be sure the League was part-time and always a complement, never a rival, to the Abbey, but it donated memorably (if fleetingly) to the Abbey repertory and, more valuably, to the imaginative well-being of Abbey actors and directors who could now occasionally get off that 'peasant treadmill' and roam about in theatrical landscapes that vastly multiplied and revitalized their skills. The discipline and labour demanded by the philosophical and psychological complexity of the League's world repertory enabled the actors to stretch their craft to maximum suppleness and to reinvigorate the staling national theatre. One critic accused the League of attracting merely a self-serving audience of 'playwrights and potential playwrights', implying Dublin-style that by pandering to special interests the League *a priori* denied any justification for its existence. Lennox Robinson once shrewdly remarked that to an Irish audience the only thing worse than a foreign play is an honest Irish one. But his uphill battle to let in a little European fresh air was so successful that the League soon had a continuing membership of nearly three hundred. It not only filled the pressing needs of Abbey actors for more varied roles, inspired 'potential playwrights' and let Dublin

19

and Yeats see Yeats's new plays, but most of all the League educated its audiences in the cultural variety and dramatic excellence which Ireland lacked, and it helped to dissipate a little the Abbey's fear that its gains were too brittle to sustain European incursion.

The League succeeded so far beyond original expectations that by 1928 there was a dependable enough demand for continental drama to encourage Micheál macLiammóir and Hilton Edwards to open the Dublin Gate Theatre, a full-time company offering an international repertory. The Gate's choice of productions was so similar to the League's that in 1929 the League phased itself out, its purpose accomplished, and League members were urged to transfer support to the Gate. There were two short-lived efforts to revive the League. In 1936, the League regrouped for two productions during a period when the Gate had run into internal troubles and had split into two companies, and the Abbey was putting on an ill-advised series of foreign plays in pathetic competition with the Gate. And then in 1941, a small corps of original League members rallied a nostalgic attempt to re-establish the group on an ongoing basis. They managed four offerings, and on 20 December 1941, the League gave its final performance.

The tradition of experiment instituted in Ireland by the League continued beyond the establishment of the Gate Theatre. In 1937, for instance, an 'Experimental Theatre' was organized by Ria Mooney with the Abbey's support. It served primarily as a testing ground for young Irish dramatists (and exists today in the basement Peacock Theatre of the new Abbey). Mooney's group performed a few European works, particularly Lorca's plays, and it attests to the duaribility of the trend introduced by the League. Today, little (or off-Abbey) theatre is alive in Dublin. The Gate, under the direction of Hilton Edwards, enjoys a long overdue official recognition in the form of a government subsidy. Thriving experimental groups like the Stanislavsky-oriented Focus and the Project Arts Theatre are the inheritors of the League's tradition, and the annual Dublin Theatre Festival has travelled on its bumpy fiscal road for over fifteen years, giving foreign companies as well as Irish ones a chance to produce a rich repertory of Irish and non-Irish work.

But the revolution in cultural consciousness fought by the League and the Gate is far from over, and, Common Market membership notwithstanding, there has been no unconditional surrender of Ireland's formidable insularity. The old prejudices of the kind Brendan Behan reduced to absurdity in *The Hostage* cling tenaciously. The Abbey today is anaemic, a state-sponsored national monument dedicated to gorgeously apparelled revivals mounted for the tourist trade. It has been a critical commonplace for years that the Abbey went into a terminal decline in the late 'thirties, one in which it still lingers; a diagnosis sadly confirmed by the fact that it is still unable to chance even an entertaining, mild little political satire like Brian Friel's *The Mundy Scheme*. Official Ireland still can't mock itself out loud, not even ever so gently. *The Playboy of the Western World* is honoured at the Synge centennial, but has any real root progress been made?

And vestiges of unfriendly suspicion towards recent foreign plays linger on. 'There's no place on earth like the world' but V. S. Pritchett in his marvellous essay on Dublin is correct when he writes that Dublin has never had much of Europe nor much feeling for it. Foreign drama there is, but only after a time lag, as if a play had to pass some safety test before it could be produced. Only on very rare occasions, like the Theatre Festival's sponsorship of the Living Theatre's *Frankenstein*, does Dublin get to see a play that is making news elsewhere. Maybe someday, when all the old political furores can raise no more than Behan's kind of reminiscent chuckle, maybe then Ireland will sustain permanently the kind of living world theatre it knew in the days of the Drama League.

A list of productions

Where programmes were unavailable, an incomplete cast was drawn from reviews, diaries and the memories of those who were involved in the Dublin Drama League.

9, 17 February; 10, 11, 12 April, 1919

THE LIBERATORS
A drama in three acts *by* Srgjan Tucic,
translated by Fanny S. Copeland

General Rashka Karastoyanoff	Fred Harford (Bernard J. Doyle)
Milada, his mother	Mrs. Kirkwood Hackett
Lyuben, his son	Michael Dolan (Philip Guiry)
Katya, his daughter	Nell Stewart
Dragolyub Bayalovitch	Eric Gorman
Sofia Popova	Christine Hayden (Dympna Daly)
Boris, her son	George Larchet (J. P. Goodall)
Dr. Nikola Markoff	Kerry Ronan
Petya Kozluhoff	Paul Farrell
Vyera Ivanova	Eileen ffrench-Mullen (Haggie Campbell)
Petkoff	F. Harford (Philip Guiry)
Gantcheff	Grattan Esmond
Hristoforoff	G. Larchet
Naumoff	F. C. McCormack (J. Hugh Nagle)
Georgi Drutchkoff	Hubert Maguire
Styanoff	Arthur Shields

Produced by Lennox Robinson

27 April, 1919

THE PRETTY SABINE WOMEN
A comedy in three acts *by* Leonid Andreyev

Scipio	Philip Guiry
Paulus	Arthur Shields
A tall, fat Roman	C. Bruce
Other Romans	Gerald Thomas, W. Ray, John Bruce, George Douglas, Barry Fitzgerald
Sabine Women:	
Cleopatra	Mrs. Kirkwood Hackett
Veronica	Haggie Campbell
Proserpine	Mary Hayes
Juno	Beatrice Elvery
Other Women	Catherine Doyle, D. Best, Majorie Elvery, Dymphna Daly
Sabine Husbands:	
Ancus Martius	Eric Gorman
Serpy's Husband	J. H. Nagle
Other Sabines	Pat J. Hayden, Valentine Young, T. V. Carroll, Myles Dillon, Liam Paul, etc.

Produced by Lennox Robinson

22

27 April, 1919

A NIGHT AT AN INN
by Lord Dunsany

A. E. Scott-Fortescue — Philip Guiry
William Jones (Bill) — F. C. McCormack
Albert Thomas — Eric Gorman
Jacob Smith (Sniggers) — Arthur Shields

Produced by Arthur Shields

7 March, 1920

THE TROJAN WOMEN
by Euripides, *translated by* Gilbert Murray

Hecuba — Maud Gonne-MacBride
Cassandra — Elizabeth Young
Pallas Athena — Christine Hayden
Andromache — Máire Nic Shiubhlaigh
Helen — Cathleen Murphy
Poseidon and Menalaus — F. J. McCormick
Talthybus — Arthur Shields

7 March, 1920

A TRAGEDIAN IN SPITE OF HIMSELF
by Anton Chekov

Tolkachov — J. A. West
Murashkin — Peter Nolan

11, 12 April, 1920

THE LIFE OF MAN
A drama in five acts *by* Leonid Andreyev

A Being in Grey Called He — Paul Ruttledge (Lennox Robinson)
Old Women — Agnese O'Higgins, Jane Foster, Mona O'Callaghan, Norah O'Neill
Doctor — Michael J. Dolan
Father of Man — F. J. McCormick
Kinspeople — Christine Hayden, Hubert McGuire, Dorothy Lynd, Sheila O'Grady
Neighbours — R. Kenny, Margaret Coughlin, J. Mahon, H. L. Corrigan, Anne Bailey
Wife of Man — Cathleen Murphy
Man — Arthur Shields
Guests — Michael J. Dolan, Peter Nolan, Lini Doran, Maureen Delany, May Craig, Eric Gorman
Servant — W. Cody
Old Servant Woman — Esme Ward
Doctor — Eric Gorman
Heirs — Christine Hayden, Dorothy Lynd, Maureen Delany

Produced by Arthur Shields

23

7, 8 November, 1920

THE LAUGHTER OF THE GODS
A tragedy in three acts *by* Lord Dunsany

King Karnos	Myles Dillon
Voice of the Gods	Paul Farrell
Ichtharion	Anthony James
Ludibras	Andrew Dillon
Harpagas	James O'Dea
First Sentry	George Lynch
Second Sentry	Theophilus Hook
One of the Camel Guard	Peter Kerley
An Executioner	John MacGrath
The Queen	Katherine MacCormack
Tharmia	Angela Coyne
Arolind	Grace MacCormack
Carolyx	Columba O'Carroll

Produced by Katherine MacCormack

7, 8 November, 1920

NO SMOKING
A farce in one act *by* Jacinto Benavente

A Lady	Helen Carter
A Young Lady	Cathleen Murphy
A Gentleman	Paul Farrell
A Conductor	J. O'Farrell

Produced by Paul Farrell

17 November, 1920

THE LAST VISIT
by Hermann Sudermann
A Dublin Drama League At Home Reading

5, 6 December, 1920

THE CASSILIS ENGAGEMENT
by St. John Hankin

Mrs. Borridge	Eva Kirkwood
Geoffrey Cassilis	Ralph Hackett
Major Warrington	Breffni O'Rourke
Ethel Borridge	Margot Brunton
Mrs. Cassilis	Eileen ffrench-Mullen
Lady Marchmont	Edith St. Faith
Countess of Remenham	Esme Ward
Lady Mabel Venning	Nano Dillon
Miss Herries	E. Stewart
The Rector	F. J. McCormick
The Maid	Helena Keily
The Butler	Jack Fay Smith

13, 14 November, 1921

THE STRONGER
by August Strindberg

Madame X	Elizabeth Young
Mademoiselle Y	Dorothy Casey

24

THE SALOON
by Henry James

Owen Wingrave	Brereton Barry
Kate Julian	Nell Stuart
Spencer Coyle	James Duncan
Bobby Lechemere	Alan Duncan
Also	Elspeth Stephens, Jessie Hill

A PERFECT DAY
by Emile Mazaud, *translated by* Esther Sutro

Trouchard	Michael Dolan
Mouton	Peter Nolan
Maid Marie	May Craig

11, 12 December, 1921

THE MARRIAGE OF COLUMBINE
by Harold Chapin

Columbine	Eileen Crowe
Scaramouche	P. J. Carolan

29, 30 January, 1922

THE BEAR
by Anton Chekov

An Aged Footman	James O'Dea

A FLORENTINE TRAGEDY
by Oscar Wilde

With   Paul Farrell, Mr. Brereton, Elizabeth Young, Katherine MacCormick, C. Perry, A. Duncan, E. Fitzgerald, G. Norman, G. Phibbs, S. Richards

THE FESTIVAL OF BACCHUS
by H. Schnitzler

19, 20 March, 1922

DIFF'RENT
A play in two acts *by* Eugene O'Neill

Captain Caleb Williams	P. J. Carolan
Emma Crosby	May Craig
Captain John Crosby	Barry Fitzgerald
Mrs. Crosby	Edith Dodd
Jack Crosby	Tony Quinn
Harriet Williams	Anne Kirby
Alfred Rogers	Hugh Nagle
Benny Rogers	Alan Duncan

Produced by Lennox Robinson

AUGUSTUS IN SEARCH OF A FATHER
by Harold Chapin

Watchman	Michael J. Dolan
Policeman	J. MacGrath
Augustus	Ralph Brereton Barry

Produced by Kathleen MacCormick

5, 6 November, 1922

THE THREE DAUGHTERS OF DUPONT
by Eugene Brieux, *translated by* St. John Hankin

M. Dupont	James O'Dea
Madame Dupont	Edith Dodd
Antonin's Wife	Margot Brunton
Antonin	Ralph Brereton Barry

Also   May Craig, C. Perry, Christine Hayden, Edith Brombell,
Shelia Richards, Gabriel Fallon, M. J. Dolan, Eric Gorman,
P. J. Carolan

Produced by Michael Dolan

3, 4 December, 1922

THE BLOT IN THE SCUTCHEON
by Robert Browning

Earl Mertoun	Gardiner Hill
Mildred Tresham	Eileen Crowe
Gerrard	Michael J. Dolan
Also	P. J. Carolan, J. Hand

Produced by Mr. Fay

THE JUBILEE
by Anton Chekov

With   Mr. O'Dea, Miss MacCormack, Mr. Dillon, Miss Coyne

11, 12 February, 1923

THE RETURN OF THE PRODIGAL
by St. John Hankin

Eustace	Brereton Barry
Lady Farrington	Harman White
Dr. Glaisher	James O'Dea
The Mother	Mona Kirkwood Hackett
The Sister	Miss Coghlan

Also   Miss White, Miss Freda Fay, Mr. Fred Jeffs, Hugh O'Neill,
Walter Bryan, Barrett MacDonnell, Jackson Dunn, H. Phillipson

26

21, 22 October, 1923

THE KINGDOM OF GOD
by Gregorio Martinez Sierra, *English version by* Helen and
Harley Granville-Barker

Old Man	Tony Quinn	Quica	Lini Doran
Gabriel	Michael J. Dolan	Sister Garcia	Eileen Crowe
Trajano	Barry Fitzgerald	Margarita	Margaret Guinness
Sister Garcia	Eileen Crowe	Enrique	F. J. McCormick
Sister Juliana	Gertrude Murphy	Sister Dionisia	Maureen Delany
Sister Manuela	Christine Hayden	Engracia	Joan Sullivan
Don Lorenzo	J. Hand	Lorenza	Pearle Moore
Maria Isabel	J. Hill Tulloch	The Innocent	Cecile Perry
Lulu	Edith Cambell	Morineto	James Shields
Liborio	Gabriel Fallon	Policarpo	Eric Gorman
Candelas	Katherine MacCormack	Vincente	P. J. Carolan
Cecilia	Beatrice Elvery	Sister Gracia	Eileen Crowe
The Dumb Girl	Shelah Richards	Paquita	Norman Joyce
Sister Cristiana	Esme Ward	Juan de Dios	Ralph Brereton Barry
Sister Feliciana	Dorothy Lynd	Felipe	Tony Quinn

Produced by Arthur Shields
Sets by Seaghan Barlow

9, 10 December, 1923

TIME IS A DREAM
A play in six scenes *by* Henri Lenormand

Nico Van Eyden	Arthur Shields	Riemke Van Eyden	Edith Dodd
Saidyah	F. J. McCormick	Mrs. Beunke	Lini Saurin
Romee Cremers	Eileen Crowe		

Produced by Arthur Shields

EVERYBODY'S HUSBAND
by Gilbert Cannan

A Girl	Shelah Richards
Her Mother	Angela Coyne
Her Grandmother	Margaret Guinness
Her Great Grandmother	Katherine MacCormack
A Maid	Judith Wilson
A Domino	Andrew Dillon

Produced by Katherine MacCormack

17, 18 February, 1924

THE HOSTAGE
A play in three acts *by* Paul Claudel, *translated by* Bryan Cooper

Pope Pius	Michael J. Dolan
Father Badilon	Barry Fitzgerald
Georges	Arthur Shields
Toussaint	F. J. McCormick
Sygne De Coufontaine	Eileen Crowe

Produced by Arthur Shields

27

30 and 31 March, 1924

AT THE HAWKS WELL *a Nō play by* W. B. Yeats
First performance in Ireland
At Home in Yeats's Residence in Merrion Square

The Hawk Girl	Eileen Magee
The Chorus Leader	Lennox Robinson
The Old Man	Frank Fay
Cuchulain	Michael J. Dolan

Costumes, Masks and Music by Edmund Dulac

27, 28 April and 10 August, 1924

HENRY IV
by Luigi Pirandello, *translated by* Edward Storer

Henry IV	Paul Ruttledge (Lennox Robinson)
Landolph	Tony Quinn
Ordulph	Gabriel Fallon
Harold	Edmund Dillon
Berthold	Barry Fitzgerald
Old Waiter	Eric Gorman
A Valet	P. J. Carolan
The Marchioness Matilda	Elizabeth Young
Frida	Ria Mooney
Marquis Charles di Nolli	Arthur Shields
Baron Tito Belcredi	F. J. McCormick
Dr. Dionysius Genomi	Michael J. Dolan

Produced by Arthur Shields

9, 10 November; 7, 8 December, 1924

THE PASSION FLOWER
A drama in three acts *by* Jacinto Benavente

Raimunda	Sara Allgood	Estaban	Sydney J. Morgan
Acacia	Shelah Richards	Norbert	F. J. McCormick
Juliana	Maureen Delaney	Faustino	P. J. Carolan
Milagros	Norma Joyce	Tio Eusebio	Gabriel Fallon
Dona Isabel	Gertrude McInery	Bernabe	Tony Quinn
Fidela	Mary McAuliffe	Rubio	Michael J. Dolan
Engracia	Maeve McMurrough	Friends	Mary Hickey, Joan
Bernabea	Gladys Monk		Harold, Kate Knowles
Gaspara	May Craig		

4, 5 January, 1925

MASSES AND MAN
by Ernst Toller, *translated by* Vera Mendel

The Woman	Dorothy Lynd
The Husband	Arthur Shields
The Nameless One	Sydney J. Morgan
The Guide	Gabriel Fallon
An Officer	T. Aye
A Priest	Michael J. Dolan
Two Prisoners	Joan Sullivan, Shelah Richards
Working Men and Women	E. Dodd, J. Tayler, M. Ross,

M. MacMorogh, J. Sullivan, S. Richards, R. Geary,
J. Dillon, R. Murphy, J. Straw, T. Aye

Produced by Arthur Shields

THE SCENE THAT WAS TO WRITE ITSELF
by George Dunning Gribble

The Wife	Margot Brunton	The Lover	Ralph Brereton Barry
The Husband	Rutherford Mayne	The Author	Gerald Fitzpatrick

Produced by Lennox Robinson

1, 2 February, 1925

THE SCHOOL FOR PRINCESSES
A comedy in three acts *by* Jacinto Benavente

King Gustavus Adolphus of Alfania	W. D. Johnston
Princess Constanza	Shelah Richards
Princess Felicia	Joyce Chancellor
Prince Maximo	Eric Gorman
Princess Eudoxia	Christine Hayden
Prince Silvio	Arthur Ward
Duke Alexander	Arthur Shields
Prince Albert of Suavia	T. Aye
The Duchess of Berlandia	Edith Dodd
The Ambassador of Suavia	G. McClinchie
The Ambassador of Franconia	L. Elyan
The Ambassadress of Franconia	Maureen Delaney
The President of the Ministry	A. Dillon
An Usher	G. McGlinchie

Produced by Lennox Robinson

15, 16 March, 1925

THE CLOISTER
by Emile Verhaeren, *translated by* Osman Edwards

Balthasar	John Stephenson	Father Thomas	William Dennis
Prior	Frank Fay	Dom Mark	Michael Enright

Produced by Frank Fay

19, 20 April, 1925

THE SPOOK SONATA
by August Strindberg

Old Hummel	Gabriel Fallon
The Student	Paul Ruttledge
The Milkmaid	Annie Evans
The Housekeeper	May Craig
The Ghost of the Consul	Arthur Shields
The Dark Lady	Joan Sullivan
The Colonel	F. J. McCormick
The Mummy	Maeve McMorrough
The Young Lady	Shelah Richards
The Dandy	Tony Quinn
Johansson	M. J. Scott
Bengtsson	P. J. Carolan
The Fiancee	Dorothy Lynd
The Cook	Christine Hayden

Produced by Arthur Shields

29

THE WEDDING MORNING
A comedy in one act by Arthur Schnitzler

Anatol	Arthur Ward	Max	Pablo Quesada
Franz	R. H. Colwill	Iona	Margot Brunton

Produced by Arthur Ward

11 July, 1925
IPHIGENIA IN TAURUS
by Euripides
Dublin Drama League At-Home

Iphigenia	Elizabeth Young
Orestes	Lennox Robinson
Pylades	Arthur Shields

29, 30 November, 1925
THE DANCE OF DEATH, PART I
by August Strindberg, *translated by* Edwin Björkman

Edgar	Paul Ruttledge	Jinny	Joan Sullivan
Alice	Maeve McMurrough	An Old Woman	Christine Hayden
Curt	Barry Fitzgerald		

Produced by Arthur Shields

24, 25 January, 1926
DR. KNOCK
A comedy in three acts *by* Jules Romains,
English version by Harley Granville-Barker

Dr. Knock	F. J. McCormick
Dr. Parpalaid	Michael J. Dolan
Mousque	Eric Gorman
Bernard	Arthur Shields
The Town Crier	Michael Scott
A Country Fellow	P. J. Carolan
Another Country Fellow	Gabriel Fallon
Scipio	Tony Quinn
Madame Parpalaid	Edith Brambell
Madame Remy	Maureen Delaney
A Farmer's Wife	Christine Hayden
Madame Pons	Helena Maloney
A Nurse	Hermone Wilson

Produced by Gabriel Fallon

14, 15 February, 1926
MAGIC
A comedy in three acts *by* G. K. Chesterton

The Duke	F. J. McCormick
Doctor Crimthorpe	Michael J. Dolan
The Rev. Cyril Smith	Eric Gorman
Morris Carleon	P. J. Carolan
Hastings	Tom Moran
The Stranger	Paul Farrell
Patricia Carleon	Mrs. D. Bannard Cogley

Produced by Gearoid O'Lochlainn

30

IN THE ZONE
by Eugene O'Neill

Smitty	Gabriel Fallon	Ivan	Tony Quinn
Davis	Tom Moran	Jack	Arthur Shields
Swanson	Michael Scott	Driscoll	P. J. Carolan
Scotty	J. Stevenson	Cocky	Michael J. Dolan

Produced by Barry Fitzgerald

14, 15 March, 1926
HEARTBREAK HOUSE
by George Bernard Shaw

Ellie Dunn	Shelah Richards
Nurse Guinness	Maureen Delany
Captain Shotover	Barry Fitzgerald
Lady Utterword	Eileen Crowe
Mr. Hushabye	F. J. McCormick
Boss Mangan	J. Stevenson
Randall Utterword	Arthur Ward
A Burglar	Gabriel Fallon

Produced by Lennox Robinson

24, 25 April, 1926
FASHIONS FOR MEN
A comedy in three acts *by* F. Molnar

Peter Juhasz	Barry Fitzgerald
Adele	Eileen Crowe
Aristocratic Lady	Christine Hayden
Oscar Mezei	P. J. Carolan
Unassuming Lady	Christine Keogh
Philip	Eric Gorman
Young Gentleman	T. Moran
Thorough Young Lady	May Craig
Dissatisfied Lady	Maureen Delaney
Nervous Gentleman	J. Stephenson
Old Gentleman	Peter Nolan
Patient Lady	Beatrice Toal
Cabman	Tony Quinn

Produced by Michael J. Dolan

29 May, 1926
THE ONLY JEALOUSY OF EMER
by William Butler Yeats

First Musician	J. Stephenson
Second Musician	E. Leeming
Third Musician	T. Moran
The Ghost of Cuchulain	F. J. McCormick
The Figure of Cuchulain	Arthur Shields
Emer	Eileen Crowe
Eithne Inguba	Shelah Richards
The Woman of the Sidhe	Norah McGuiness

Masks and Costumes by Norah McGuiness

31

THE CAT AND THE MOON
by William Butler Yeats

1st Musician	J. Stephenson	A Blind Beggar	P. J. Carolan
2nd Musician	Lennox Robinson	A Lame Beggar	Michael J. Dolan
3rd Musician	T. Moran		

31 July, 1926
CYCLOPS
by Euripides
At Home

Cyclops	Rutherford Mayne
Ulysses	Denis Johnston

24, 25 October, 1926
THE PLEASURE OF HONESTY
by Luigi Pirandello, translated by Arthur Livingstone

Angelo Baldovino	Paul Farrell
Agatha Renni	Shelah Richards
La Signora Maddalena	Eileen Crowe
Marquis Setti	Michael J. Dolan
A Clergyman	J. Stephenson
Marchetto Fongi	P. J. Carolan
Four Directors of the Board	Tony Quinn, C. Pilkington, E. Keatings, M. Scott
A Maid	Hermione Wilson
A Butler	Walter Dillon
A Nurse	Maureen Delany

Produced by Gabriel Fallon

28, 29 November, 1926
THE DANCE OF DEATH, PART II
by August Strindberg

Edgar, Captain of the Coast Artillery	Paul Ruttledge
Alice	Maeve McMurrough
Curt	Barry Fitzgerald
Allan	Charles Pilkington
Judith	Shelah Richards
The Lieutenant	Arthur Shields

Produced by Shelah Richards and Beatrice Campbell

THE HOUSETOP MADMAN
by Kwan Kikuchi

Yoshitaro Katsushima	Gabriel Fallon	Kikhiji	Tony Quinn
Sae Jiro	Lyle Donaghy	Hag	V. Flemming-Moran
Gisuke	Edgar F. Keating	Tosaku	P. J. Carolan
Oyoshi	Edith Dodd		

Produced by Beatrice Campbell and Shelah Richards
Designed by Beatrice Campbell

12 December, 1926

THE DEAR DEPARTING
by Leonid Andreyev

Policeman	Michael Scott
Another Policeman	H. D. Walsh
A Lady	Gertrude McEnery
Nelly	Biddy Campbell
English Tourist	T. Purefoy
His Friend	F. W. Koenigs
A Bloodthirsty Lady	Edith Dodd
A Photographer	H. D. Walsh
A Russian Tourist	Andrew Dillon
Dasha	Kitty Curling
Masha	Mary Manning
Kasha	Hermione Wilson
Drunken Man	Charles Tinsley
A Special Correspondent	G. Burke Kennedy
A Landlord	Charles Tinsley

Produced by Katherine MacCormack

POOR JOHN
by Gregorio Martinez-Sierra (acted by Dramik)

Mama Pepa	Edith Dodd	Antonio	T. A. Purefoy
Mama Inez	Madeline Ross	Maid	Hermione Wilson
Marciana	Evelyn Vigors	1st Factory Hand	Charles Pilkington
Don John	Soames	2nd Factory Hand	Edgar Keatings

Produced by Dorothy Lynd

16, 17 January, 1927

EMPEROR JONES
by Eugene O'Neill

An Old Native Woman	Joan Sullivan
Henry Smithers	John Stevenson
Brutus Jones	Rutherford Mayne
Jeff	Arthur Shields
Three Negro Convicts	F. W. Koenigs, C. W. Tinsley, C. T. Culhane
The Prison Guard	M. MacNamara
Planters	Evelyn Vigors, C. Sherlock, W. Scott, H. D. Walshe, T. O'Connell
The Auctioneer	W. J. Tunney
The Slaves	Edgar Keatings, Joan Sullivan, G. Burke Kennedy
The Singing Negroes	M. MacNamara, C. T. Culhane, C. W. Tinsley, F. W. Koenigs, T. Kennedy
The Witch Doctor	Michael Scott

Produced by L. Robinson
Sets by Dorothy Travers-Smith

33

TRIFLES
by Susan Glaspell

Mrs. Peters	May Craig
Mrs. Hale	Eileen Crowe
George Henderson	F. J. McCormick
Henry Peters	Tony Quinn
Lewis Hale	M. J. Dolan

Produced by P. J. Carolan

20, 21 March, 1927

DON JUAN
by James Elroy Flecker

Don Juan	Robert Bilton	Charley	T. Purefoy
Don Pedro	Eric Gorman	His Friend	C. H. Pilkington
Lord Framlingham	Paul Farrell	A Little Girl	K. Curling
Lady Isabel	Mary Manning	Her Mother	Christine Hayden
Lady Ann	Shelah Richards	Bob Evans	Peter Nolan
Owen Jones	J. Stevenson	Mary	May Carey
Harree	T. O'Connell	Bill	Barry Fitzgerald
Tisbea	Ria Mooney	A Hungry Man	Gabriel Fallon
		A Policeman	Michael Scott

Produced by Lennox Robinson

24, 25 April, 1927

THE CRADLE SONG
by Gregorio Martinez-Sierra

The Prioress	Sybil le Brocquy
The Vicaress	May Carey
The Mistress of Novices	K. McManus
Sister Maria Jesus	Geraldine Leeson
Sister Inez	Dorothy Day
Sister Torners	Marion Ross
Sister Joanna of the Cross	Ann Dewhallow
Sister Sagrario	Betty Chancellor
Sister Marcella	Maisie Ruscelli
Teresa	Caitlin Sherlock
The Doctor	N. J. Tunney
Antonio	C. Culhane

Produced by Mrs. Hill-Tulloch

THE STRANGER
by Perez Hirschbein, *translated from the Yiddish by* Etta Block

Mordcha Gadaliah	Lawrence Elyan
Fraidelle	Rachel Jaffe
An Old Woman	Florence M. Barron

Produced by Arthur Shields

34

29, 30 May, 1927
CAESAR AND CLEOPATRA
by George Bernard Shaw

Caesar	F. J. McCormick
Cleopatra	Maisie Ruscelli
Belzanor	G. J. Moran
Persian	G. Green
Nubian Sentinel	M. Finn
Bel Affris	M. Scott
Guardsman	W. Dillon
Ftatateet	Maureen Delany
Pothinus	Gabriel Fallon
Theodutus	L. Elyan
Achillas	Arthur Shields
Rufio	J. Stephenson
Brittanus	Eric Gorman
Lucious Septimus	P. J. Carolan
Centurion	Peter Nolan
Ptolemy Dionysius	M. Nolan
Wounded Roman Soldier	W. Allgood
Apollodorus	W. J. Crawley
Roman Sentinel	G. Burke Kennedy
Slave Girl	Mary Manning
Musician	A. Brown
Charmian	Ria Mooney
Irish	May Craig
Priest	M. Scott
1st Official and Major Domo	S. Eliasoff
Second Official	U. Wright

Produced by Michael J. Dolan
Sets by Dorothy Travers-Smith

30, 31 October, 1927
HE WHO GETS SLAPPED
by Leonid Andreyev, *translated by* Gregory Zilboorg

Polly	M. Scott
Tilly	W. Scott
Briquet	P. J. Carolan
Mancini	Eric Gorman
He	Paul Ruttledge
Jackson	J. Stephenson
Consuelo	Kitty Curling
Bezano	Gilbert Green
Baron Regnard	Rutherford Mayne
A Gentleman	Kerry Ronan
Thomas	Peter Nolan
Waiter	T. Moran
Conductor	Gabriel Fallon
Circus Performers	Gertrude Quinn, Hazel Ellis, U. Wright, M. Clarke, J. Loughrey

Produced by Arthur Shields

35

27, 28 November, 1927
THE GAME AS HE PLAYED IT
by Luigi Pirandello

Leone Gala	J. Stevenson
Silia	Merial Moore
Guido Venanzi	E. W. Tocher
Doctor Spiga	T. Purefoy
Filippo	P. J. Carolan
Barelli	A. J. Leventhal
The Marchesino Mighliorita	Arthur Shields
Drunken Swell	C. H. Pilkington
Another Drunken Swell	Alan Duncan
A Third Drunken Swell	Brian O'Donoghue
Clara	May Craig

Produced by Lennox Robinson

22, 23 January, 1928
A COMEDY OF GOOD AND EVIL
by Richard Hughes

Rev. John Williams	J. Stephenson
Minnie	May Craig
Gladys	Kitty Curling
Scraggy Evan	M. Clarke
Owain Flatfish	P. J. Carolan
Mari Bakehouse	G. Quinn
Mrs. Bakehouse	Christine Hayden
Timothy	T. Moran
Mr. Jones	Eric Gorman
Mrs. Ressurection	Maureen Delany

Produced by P. J. Carolan

18, 19 March, 1928
THE FATHER
by August Strindberg, *translated by* C. D. Jocock

Captain	Paul Ruttledge	The Nurse	May Carey
Laura	Eileen Crowe	Bertha	Kitty Curling
The Pastor	Michael J. Dolan	Nojd	E. W. Tocher
The Doctor	John Stevenson	The Batman	P. J. Carolan

Produced by Barry Fitzgerald

6, 8 May, 1928
THE FOUNTAIN
by Eugene O'Neill

Ibnu Aswad	Frederick W. Koenigs
Juan Ponce de Leon	Tom Moran
Pedro	P. J. Carolan
Maria	Eileen Crowe
Luis de Alvaredo	J. Stephenson
Yusef	Henry Benedict
Diego	Lal Canfield

36

Vincente de Cordova	Kerry Ronan
Alonzode Oviedo	R. Charles
Manuel de Castillo	M. Batchen
Christoval de Mendoza	Michael Scott
Columbus	Arthur Shields
Firar Quesada	A. J. O'Farrell
Nano	A. Dillon
Beatris de Cordova	Shelah Richards
The Indian Chief	Henry Savage
The Medicine Man	Michael Scott
The Father Superior	Kerry Ronan
The Nephew	Henry Benedict

Produced by Denis Johnston
Indian dance arranged by Sarah Patrick

10, 11 February, 1929
THE THREE SISTERS
by Anton Chekov

Olga	Marian Tennant	Andrey	Fred Johnson
Irina	B. Chancellor	Verschinin	Paul Farrell
Masha	Merie Moore	Natasha	Kate Curling
Tusenbach	Tom Moran	Solyony	Henry Benedict
Chebutykin	Gabriel Fallon	Ferapont	Havilan Jackson
Kuligin	J. Stephenson		

Produced by Dorothy Day

10, 11 March, 1929
HOPPLA!
by Ernst Toller

Karl Thomas	A. J. Leventhal
Albert Kroll	R. Charles
Wilheim Kilman	Jack Dwan
Eva Berg	Shelah Richards
Mrs. Meller	Blanaid O'Carroll
Rand	Michael J. Clark
Lt. Baron Friedrich	Henry Benedict
Professor Ludin	Frank O'Connor
Financier	James Layne
Financier's Son	Charles Ashdown
Pickel	Gerald Little
War Ministers	B. V. D. Jemmer
Count Lande	Charles Kenyon
Mrs. Kilman	Dorothy Day
Lotte Kilman	Hermione Wilson
Fritz	Raymond Fardy
Grete	Una Fardy
1st Election Officer	A. Dillon
2nd Election Officer	Charles Ashdown
Student	J. B. O'Mahony
Head Waiter	John Patchell
Page Boy	Edward Raymond
Wireless Operator	Henry Benedict
Porter	M. Finn
Chief of Police	A. Dillon
Examining Judge	B. V. D. Jemmer

Produced by E. W. Tocher (Denis Johnston)
Designed by H. Kernoff

28 April, 1929
MASQUE OF VENICE
by Gribble

12, 13 May, 1929
GIVE A DOG
by Lennox Robinson

Mrs. Enright	Maureen Delany
Mrs. Barrett	Eileen Crowe
Philip Barrett	Paul Ruttledge
Mayor Barrett	Rutherford Mayne
James Clarke	John Stephenson
Dolores de Kuypers	Shelah Richards
Milly Wheaton	Betty Chancellor
Doctor Pobjoy	Barry Fitzgerald
Hayden	Michael Scott
Collins	P. J. Carolan
Bruce	Arthur Shields
Muriel Clarke	Rachel Law

19, 20 January, 1936
in the Torch Theatre
HIS WIDOW'S HUSBAND
by Jacinto Benevente

Zurita	T. Purefoy	Eudocia	Margaret Mullins
Carolina	Clodagh Barrett	Casalonga	Ken Barton
Florencia	Austin Meldon	Valdiviesco	Frank Carey
Paquita	Nancy O'Doherty		

ORPHEUS
by Jean Cocteau

Euridice	Esmé Biddle
Orpheus	Brian Hughes
The Horse	Dermot Thompson
Death	Hester Plunket
Raphael	Anthony Hanson
Azrael	Richard Hanson
The Postman	Frank Carey
The Commissioner of Police	J. Hand
The Scrivener	Ken Barton

Produced by Shelah Richards and Lennox Robinson

29, 30 March, 1936
At the Gate Theatre
HOTEL UNIVERSE
by Philip Barry

Ann Field	Shelah Richards
Pat Farley	Tom Purefoy
Lily Malone	Dorothy Lowry
Alice Kendall	Charlotte McClenaghan
Norman Rose	Laurence Elyan

38

Tom Ames	Kenneth Barton
Hope Ames	Ria Mooney
Felix	Cecil Monson
Stephen Field	Robert Hennessy

Produced by Lennox Robinson

1, 2 April, 1936

ARMLET OF JADE
by Lord Longford

Yang Kuei-Fei	Ria Mooney
Prime Minister	Edward Lexy
Emperor of China	Robert Hennessy

Settings by Sheila May

15, 16, 17 December, 1941

THE FAMILY REUNION
by T. S. Eliot

Lord Monchensey	Robert Mooney
Amy	Marjorie Williams
Agatha	Shelah Richards
Ivy	Rita O'Dea
Violet	Louise Hutton
The Hon. Charles Piper	James Dunne
Hon. Gerald Piper	Tom Purefoy
Mary	Mona Sayers
Dinman	Joan Gorman
Downing	Norman Barrs
Dr. Warburton	Gerald Healy
Sargeant Winchell	Edgar Keating

Produced by Seán O'Meadhra

8–13 December, 1941
At the Gate Theatre

THE STATUE'S DAUGHTER
by Frank O'Connor

Johnny Douglas	John O'Gorman
The Rev. Walter Humphreys	Edward Keatinge
Peter Humphreys	Tom Purefoy
Joan Lathan	Kitty Thuillier
Peter Paul Sweeney	John MacDarby
Jack Costello	Alan Desmond (Michael Walshe)
Phil Doyle	Sheila Manahan
George O'Leary	Seumas Healy
Fintan O'Leary	Gerard Healy
Brigid O'Rourke	Josephine Fitzgerald
Ellen O'Rourke	Sheila Ward
Maid	Joan MacAuliffe

Produced by Michael Farrell
Assisted by Evelyn MacNeice

WOZZECK

by Georg Buchner, *translated by* Michael Walsh

Wozzeck	Dennis Barry
Marie	Gervaise Mathews
Lieutenant	Hamlyn Benson
Margaret	Louise Hutton
Andres	Jon Haerem
Doctor	Harry Brogan
Showman	James Dunne
First Spectator	John King
Second Spectator	Edmond Stewart
The Ape	Joseph Farrell
The Ass	Donal McBrien_Gus Hackett
Drum Major	Aiden Grennell
Soldier	Charles Enders
An Idiot	Seumas O'Donnell
Jew	J. MacCollum
Peasant	James Dunne
First Citizen	James O'Brien
Second Citizen	James O'Brien
Old Woman Landlady	Florence Lynch
Ballet	Christine du Boulay, Patricia Kinneen, Michael Mathews, Seumas O'Donnell
Children	Joyce Lingard, Alexis Milne, Marjorie Malin, Joan Pigot, Doreen Ryan

Produced and designed by Michael Walsh

SCARECROW OVER THE CORN

by Blanaid Salkeld

The Friend	Gerard Healy
The Scarecrow	Michael Walsh
The Girl	Sheila May
The Sitter	Wilfrid Brambell
Six Critics of the Sun	Charles Enders, Cecil Ford, Robert Mooney, Edmond Stewart, Norman Barrs, James Dunne
Four Victims of Wealth	Robert Mooney, Norman Barrs, James Dunne, Edgar Keatinge
Old Woman	Josephine Fitzgerald
Old Man	James Dunne

Produced by Shelah Richards
Designed by Louis le Brocquy
Movement by Cepta Cullen